Avoid working in the Forbidden City

Written by
Jacqueline Morley

Illustrated by
David Antram

Created and designed by
David Salariya

The Danger Zone

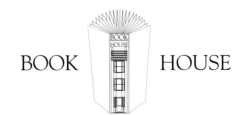

BOOK HOUSE

Contents

Author:
Jacqueline Morley studied English at
Oxford University. She has taught English and
History, and now works as a freelance writer.
She has written historical fiction and non-fiction
for children.

Artist:
David Antram was born in Brighton, England,
in 1958. He studied at Eastbourne College of Art
and then worked in advertising for fifteen years
before becoming a full-time artist. He has
illustrated many children's non-fiction books.

Series creator:
David Salariya was born in Dundee, Scotland.
He has illustrated a wide range of books and has
created and designed many new series for
publishers in the UK and overseas. In 1989 he
established The Salariya Book Company. He lives
in Brighton with his wife, illustrator Shirley Willis,
and their son Jonathan.

Editor: **Stephen Haynes**

Editorial Assistant: **Mark Williams**

Published in Great Britain in 2008 by
Book House, an imprint of
The Salariya Book Company Ltd
25 Marlborough Place, Brighton BN1 1UB
www.salariya.com
www.book-house.co.uk

HB ISBN-13: 978-1-905638-56-7
PB ISBN-13: 978-1-905638-57-4

S A L A R I Y A

1 3 5 7 9 8 6 4 2

A CIP catalogue record for this book is available
from the British Library.

Printed and bound in China.
Printed on paper from sustainable sources.

Visit our website at **www.book-house.co.uk**
for **free** electronic versions of:
You Wouldn't Want to be an Egyptian Mummy!
You Wouldn't Want to be a Roman Gladiator!
Avoid Joining Shackleton's Polar Expedition!
Avoid Sailing on a 19th-Century Whaling Ship!

Introduction

The Forbidden City – what a name! It doesn't sound the friendliest place to work in, does it? Today it's a major tourist attraction in the Chinese capital, Beijing, but for five centuries it was home to the emperors of China. Part royal dwelling and part government headquarters, it was a vast assemblage of palaces, temples and offices. It really was 'forbidden' to ordinary citizens. Only officials could enter its closely guarded walls.

The emperors were greatly feared. They could put you to death without thinking twice. Yet lots of people wanted to work for them. So let's suppose it's around 1750 and you're an ambitious young Chinese. Would you really enjoy life in the Forbidden City?

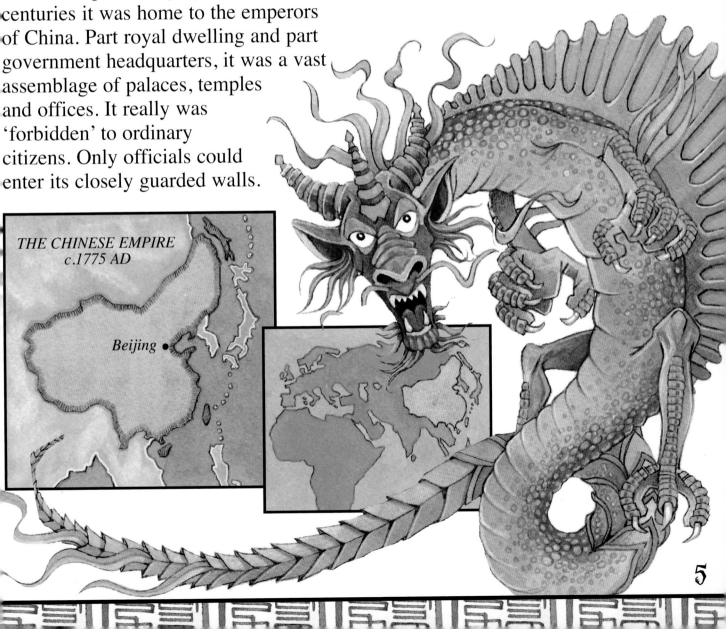

THE CHINESE EMPIRE c.1775 AD

Beijing •

Outside the gate

A poor boy gets his chance

AT SCHOOL you were always one of the brightest in your class and very hard-working. The Inspector of Schools was impressed by you.

YOUR PARENTS couldn't afford to keep you at school, but the Inspector persuaded a rich merchant to pay for you to study for the state exams.

NOW, while your friends go out to work, you study the works of Confucius, and write essays.

You live in the lively Chinese part of Beijing, outside the Ch'ien Men gate. Most Chinese have to live here, unless they are important officials. The rest of the city is for the Manchus, a people from the north who have conquered China. They've kept the best places and jobs for themselves. They distrust the Chinese, and the Chinese resent them. The Chinese hate being made to follow Manchu customs such as shaving your forehead and wearing your hair in a pigtail.

Come on, I haven't got all day!

I have.

You plan to pass enough exams to become a top official, with an office in the Imperial City. You will get to see the Forbidden City itself!

Handy hint

If you can't bear to wear a pigtail, shave your whole head and say you're a monk.

■ *Forbidden City*
□ *Imperial City*

YOU ARE HERE →

□ *Tartar or Inner City*
■ *Chinese or Outer City*

The Ch'ien Men gate is the main entrance to the Tartar or Inner City, where Manchu citizens live. It is protected by a moat and massive stone walls.

The city of the Ming

Before the Manchus came, China was ruled by the Ming dynasty. Some of the Ming were able rulers, but many were heartless, pleasure-seeking or weak. But at least they were Chinese. The most famous was the Yongle* Emperor, the third of the Ming dynasty. He was a brilliant ruler, but ruthlessly cruel. On overthrowing the rightful heir, he moved his capital to Beijing, and in 1406 he began work on creating a setting that would be fit for the emperor of the entire world – that's how China's emperors saw themselves.

Pronounce it 'Yong-lay'.

The city is outwardly much the same today.

KEY
1 Meridian Gate
2 Gate of Supreme Harmony
3 Hall of Supreme Harmony
4 Hall of Perfect Harmony
5 Hall of Preserving Harmony
6 Gate of Heavenly Purity
7 Palace of Heavenly Purity

Yongle's creation has over 9,000 rooms. Vast courtyards lead to three great halls in which the Emperor conducts state affairs. The dwelling areas behind are closed to everyone but the imperial family and their army of servants.

Now that's what I call a nice little place.

Handy hint

Don't build too high. Roofs must not interrupt the flight of spirits, who like to travel about 30 metres up.

Tales of the Ming

'UPROOTING the creeping vine' is Yongle's term for killing not only his critics but their families, friends, pupils and servants.

ON THEIR DEATHS, three of the Ming emperors had their wives killed and buried with them.

A MAN who tried to claim the Ming throne was imprisoned under a copper jar and roasted alive.

THE MING EMPERORS travelled in gilded chariots drawn by elephants with jewelled trappings.

18 PALACE MAIDS bungled an attempt to strangle their hated emperor in bed. The knot wouldn't tighten. Don't ask what happened to them!

The triumph of the Manchus

Your present emperor, known as the Qianlong* Emperor, prides himself on being a Manchu – one of the warlike people from the north who toppled the Ming dynasty in 1644. These new rulers call themselves the Qing** (pure) dynasty. They think the Chinese are far too soft-living, but they've kept to Chinese ways of running the country, because they know that without the skills of the Chinese the empire would crumble. And they've kept the lavish grandeur of the Ming court. The emperor can only be approached according to strict rules. From a golden throne (one of many), which must face south, he presides over the most rigid court ceremonies. Behind him, an elaborate gold screen protects his sacred presence from the evil influences of the north.

*Pronounce it 'Chee-an-long'.
**'Ching'.

THE KOWTOW (rhymes with 'now') is a respectful bow in which the forehead strikes the floor.

NO PEEKING! If the Emperor's procession passes through Beijing, people must shutter their windows and stay indoors. He is too sacred to be looked at.

Come away from that window!

STAMP OF APPROVAL.
All the Emperor's written orders are stamped with his gold seal. An official who receives one must obey instantly, even if it requires his own death.

Seal

Impression of the seal

Handy hint

Advice to emperors: Don't reveal whom you want as heir, or he may grab your throne. Name him on a sealed paper, to be read on your death.

There you are, sir – ready when you are!

THE EMPEROR likes to consult his ministers on state matters, but those with unwelcome opinions may be executed.

ONE OFFICIAL was so anxious when summoned by the Emperor that he ordered his coffin before setting out for the palace.

11

The Emperor's officials

t times when you've studied so hard that you can't sleep, you often take a dawn walk. That is the time when you see officials setting off for the Forbidden City to report to the Emperor at his early-morning council. Here comes an official of the fourth grade. You can tell that by the emblem on the square on his chest and the colour of the button on his hat. How important he looks as he strides out of his house to his waiting litter! A servant lights the way, and another follows with his portfolio of papers. You would love to be like him. People with official jobs have influence and can do favours, so everyone respects them and offers them gifts.

The Emperor has a vast civil service with three Grand Secretaries and six Ministries. Within these there are nine grades of civil officials and another nine of military officials. They must all dress in exactly the same way, apart from their hat button and the distinguishing emblem on their chest and back.

Handy hint

Only chief ministers get a cushion to kneel on, so if you're not in the top grade, knee pads are the answer.

I've been up all night writing this.

I'll look at it later.

THOUGH HE MAY TREMBLE before the Emperor, an official is king in his own office. His secretary humbly presents a draft report to him.

Mind the step, Your Excellency.

ALL OFFICIALS must enter the Forbidden City by a heavily guarded side gate. Once inside, they must dismount and walk; only the Emperor and his family may ride there. The gatekeeper expects a tip from everyone he lets pass. This is known as the gate 'squeeze'.

Who goes there?

AFTER A LONG WAIT in a chilly waiting room, the official finally kneels on the cold stone pavement of the Gate of Heavenly Purity, where the Emperor is seated for his dawn council.

13

Exams, exams, exams!

Jostled and pushed by desperate candidates, you're waiting for your name to appear in the results posted up outside the examination building in Beijing. You passed the local and provincial exams, but this is the crucial one – the metropolitan exam held every three years in the capital. Scholars from all over China take it, but only the very best pass. The exam doesn't test general knowledge. You're judged entirely on your ability to comment on ancient philosophical texts, and you must answer in the form of an 'eight-legged' essay, using eight headings and only 700 characters. Have your years of practice paid off?

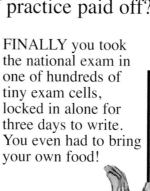

I don't feel very well.

YOUR FIRST STEP was the yearly exams in your local prefecture. Here you are handing in your paper. Then came the much more important provincial exam.

FINALLY you took the national exam in one of hundreds of tiny exam cells, locked in alone for three days to write. You even had to bring your own food!

Well?

IF YOU PASS the local exam, you are qualified to teach. If you do badly, you get a beating.

YOU PASSED the provincial exam – a major step up the career ladder. Gleeful friends escort you home.

15

A state appearance

Congratulations! You passed the metropolitan exams and are now a junior official in the Board of Censors. Your duties include seeing that everyone obeys the rigid rules of positioning and behaviour that govern state events. Today is one of the most important: the Emperor's dawn appearance in the Hall of Supreme Harmony to welcome the New Year.

Your job, on this icy early morning, is to marshal thousands of officials into lines, according to rank. There are markers on the pavement to help you. The lamps and incense burners are lit and the musicians ready, awaiting the great moment. The Emperor will enter the hall by a rear door. Officials and guests who have been shivering for hours in the courtyard won't even get a glimpse of him – at such times he is too sacred to be seen. Within the hall, a canopy shields him even from the top people who are allowed near the throne. Outside, a master of ceremonies tells the crowd when to kneel, when to stand and when to kowtow.

REPORT anyone who has a hat on askew or talks loudly to his neighbour during the long wait. They will have their pay docked.

I **am** standing up straight.

16

Handy hint

Foreign envoys should never bring an odd number of gifts. Odd numbers are associated with the dead, and will be refused.

But surely we should be in front of those?

You should be behind these.

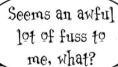

Seems an awful lot of fuss to me, what?

UP SINCE MIDNIGHT and blue with cold! Coughs and snuffles are not allowed, so hold your breath if you feel a sneeze coming.

DURING STATE FESTIVALS all other business is put on hold. Envoys from Russia, Korea, Holland, England and many other places are just left to hang around.

The Bannermen

The Manchu pride themselves on being more warlike than the Chinese (who still regard them as barbarians). In their homelands they were organised in warrior clans. The Qing emperors are keen to keep this fighting spirit alive, especially since the Chinese population far outnumbers the Manchu. They have created units of highly trained Manchu warriors who are always in command over Chinese troops. They are known as the Bannermen, because they fight under the banners of the old clans. They form a military aristocracy and have a lot of power. As a Chinese, you would be wise not to make an enemy of a Bannerman.

No-one gets past us.

COLOUR-CODED. The eight Banner units guard the Forbidden City by colour: the two yellow banners in the north, white in the east, red in the west, and blue in the South.

Bannerman in parade armour   *Imperial guards in yellow jackets*

Handy hint

Trainee archers, be warned! If you don't wear a thumb ring, the bow-string will slice into your thumb when it springs back.

Gulp!

A VICTORIOUS GENERAL presents captives to the Emperor, who watches the ceremony from the terrace of the Meridian Gate.

THE EMPEROR'S BODYGUARDS are all Bannermen. It is a great honour to be an imperial guard, as the Emperor's safety is in your hands.

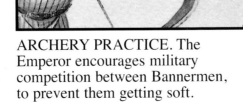

ARCHERY PRACTICE. The Emperor encourages military competition between Bannermen, to prevent them getting soft.

Show-off!

THE BANNERMEN are outstanding horsemen. Their acrobatic displays are a favourite entertainment of the Emperor.

The Emperor's day

The Emperor is in his study, composing a poem to the moon. This is how he likes to relax after a hard day's work. He gets up before daybreak and receives officials from dawn onwards. After a meal at 8 a.m., he studies the local government reports that pour in daily, holds a meeting with his household officials, and then discusses affairs of state with the ministers of his Grand Council. He has his second meal at 2 p.m. In the afternoon he turns to things of the mind: philosophy and poetry. But don't imagine he has a soft spot for poets! If he thinks a poem is slanderous, he will execute the poet and his family too – and he's ordered thousands of books to be destroyed. He always eats alone, but if he summons a concubine at night he might invite her to a meal before bedtime. She must not sit in his presence, so she eats standing up.

THE EMPEROR has his meals served wherever he fancies. Even when he takes a walk, servants follow with food and a portable stove.

HE IS SERVED boiled duck and bean curd, swallow's-nest soup and bamboo-stuffed dumplings. Everything is sampled first by his taster, in case of poison.

SWEET DREAMS? Not always! Some emperors sleep in a different bed each night, for fear of assassination.

HUNTING is part of the Emperor's schedule, too. It helps promote Manchu warrior sports. Hare hunting is a particular favourite.

What was that?

Says who?

Handy hint

Never go in a boat when you've eaten swallows. They're the favourite snack of water dragons, who'll gobble you to get at them.

A masterpiece, even if I say so myself.

PAPERWORK. Officials sort hundreds of reports daily for the Emperor to comment on. He marks them in red ink, which only he may use. He also gets secret reports passed directly to him by informants.

Empresses and concubines

There is one part of the Forbidden City you will never see. No man is allowed into the district where the Emperor lives. The workers there are all women or eunuchs. The family is ruled by the Dowager Empress, the Emperor's mother (it is a sacred duty to put parents first). Next comes the Empress – the Emperor's chief wife – then eight ranks of lesser wives, or concubines. Any of their sons can be chosen as heir, so the Dowager Empress could be a low-grade concubine and yet have authority over the Empress, who is always a noblewoman. Not a recipe for peace and quiet!

Jewelled nail protectors

LONG FINGERNAILS are a status symbol for Manchu ladies.

MANCHU WOMEN do not bind their feet like the Chinese, but shoes with a central heel give them a teetering walk.

Dowager Empress

Empress

I don't trust that little one.

You don't trust anyone.

> You'll do.

THE DOWAGER EMPRESS selects the concubines, always from Banner families. It is an honour to be chosen.

IDLE HANDS. Apart from bearing sons, the Emperor's womenfolk have nothing much to do. They pass the time with games, handicrafts and chatter.

Handy hint

Palace eunuchs love plotting, but don't get involved. If it goes wrong, you and all your friends and family will pay with your lives.

PALACE FEUDS can be deadly. One dowager empress who found her son's favourite concubine a nuisance had her pushed down a narrow well in a courtyard of the Forbidden City.

> I wish I could hear what they're saying.

CONCUBINES are prisoners for life. They cannot leave the Forbidden City even when the Emperor tires of them, to ensure that no woman belonging to him can be touched by another man.

Maidservant   *Concubines*

APRIL, with its strong winds, is the time for kite-flying contests. There are kites of all shapes: birds, fish, insects, bats, even people.

A LAVISH FIREWORK DISPLAY forms the backdrop to most of the Emperor's festivities – and to ordinary people's, too.

PRIVATE PLEASURES. The Emperor likes to invite scholarly guests to his garden, to compete with him in composing verses.

PRIVATE THEATRES in the Forbidden City entertain the Emperor's family and honoured guests.

Festivities

You're attending one of the Emperor's great feasts: the midwinter skating display and outdoor banquet. Archers give a fantastic show, hitting targets at high speed. The Emperor is snug inside his luxury sledge, but the audience is frozen to the bone. You eat on the icy ground. No-one dares mention that the food is barely warm despite the efforts of servants with portable stoves.

Handy hint

Evil spirits can only fly in straight lines, so a screen inside each gate will keep them out.

Imperial sledge

Yesss!! I hope His Majesty saw that shot!

When Heaven is displeased

This year's Festival of Lanterns is a disaster. A silk lantern catches fire, the wind fans the flames and sets the Emperor's home, the Palace of Heavenly Purity, ablaze. People panic, not knowing what to do. The Beijing firemen cannot be called out, because they lack the rank to put out an imperial fire. Such calamities are a sign that Heaven is displeased with the way things are being run on earth. Since the Emperor rules everything, he is responsible, and must put things right through rituals and prayer. But in his turn he will hold *you* responsible for any disaster in your area of work. One official's career was ended when he was blamed for a plague of locusts.

THE WATER SUPPLY for the Forbidden City is kept in bronze vessels without any taps, and the only firefighting equipment is little hand pumps – not a lot of use!

EUNUCHS RUSH to save rare porcelain and other priceless objects from the imperial treasure house. Later, it is found that many things have mysteriously disappeared.

Handy hint

Chinese dragons are fierce but not evil, and bring water, not fire. Figures of them on the roof help protect a building from burning.

Heaven help us!

We do hereby decree...

HERE WE GO AGAIN. This is not the first time the Forbidden City has caught fire. Built of wood, it easily becomes a torch. The Emperor announces immediate rebuilding.

EARTHQUAKES, often with tremors lasting for days, are another peril of life in the Forbidden City. For fear of buildings collapsing, terrified courtiers camp in tents in the courtyards.

Duty and respect

The Emperor is ploughing a ritual furrow with a golden plough, at the spring Festival of Agriculture. All year round he performs ceremonies like this, in honour of the Heavens, the Earth, the Sun, the Moon, and many other gods. This is how he fulfils his sacred duty of keeping the world in harmony with the Supreme Being.

AT THE ALTAR of Agriculture, the Emperor prays to its god, Xiannong,* the legendary inventor of agriculture and founder of Chinese civilisation. He offers him food, drink, silk and jade.

*Pronounce it 'She-an-nong'.

ANCESTOR WORSHIP is another sacred duty. The Emperor bows before the enthroned wooden tablets that represent them.

Each year you attend these rituals, standing, kneeling and kowtowing endlessly as required. By now you are the perfect Chinese civil servant, never speaking your mind, never doing anything unexpected, dreading the Emperor and distrusting everyone. How are you enjoying the job?

Handy hint

From an emperor's edict on proper conduct: 'Honour your parents and pay your taxes promptly.'

Every year the same old thing...

OLD PEOPLE must always be shown the greatest respect, the Chinese believe. To mark his 60th birthday, the Emperor gives a Feast of the Elders. Old men from all over China are invited to a banquet in the Forbidden City.

Glossary

Censors Officials responsible for checking up on other officials.

Character A written sign standing for a sound, syllable or whole word. Chinese writing has thousands of different characters.

Clan A group of related families.

Concubine A wife of lower status than the main or 'first' wife, in countries where men are allowed to have more than one wife.

Confucius A Chinese philosopher (551–479 BC) whose teachings on duty and right behaviour are still important in Chinese thought.

Dowager A widow who is allowed to keep her late husband's title. In Imperial China, the Emperor's mother had the title of Dowager Empress, even if she was not an empress but only a concubine when her husband was alive.

Dynasty A succession of rulers of the same or related families.

Edict A command or proclamation from a ruler.

Emblem A sign or badge that has some special meaning.

Envoy An official sent by one ruler to another, to deliver a message or to discuss matters affecting both countries, such as trade.

Eunuch A castrated man.

Grand Council A group of advisors to the Emperor, similar to the cabinet in modern governments. The heads of the six Ministries – Civil Office, Rites, Revenue, War, Punishments and Public Works – were members.

Grand Secretaries The emperor's three chief advisors. He received their advice separately from that of the Grand Council, and did not allow the two bodies to meet together.

Imperial Belonging to the Emperor.

Kowtow A kneeling bow, in which the forehead is touched to the ground three times.

Litter A seat resting on horizontal poles, carried by bearers.

Manchu A non-Chinese people who overthrew the Ming Dynasty and founded the Qing Dynasty.

Metropolitan Belonging to a capital city.

Ming The dynasty of emperors who ruled China from 1368 to 1644.

Portfolio A large flat case for carrying documents.

Prefecture The district administered by a local government official known as a prefect. A Chinese province contained several prefectures.

Qing (pronounced 'Ching') The dynastic name of the Manchu Emperors. The Qing Dynasty ruled China from 1644 to 1911.

Ritual A sacred act or ceremony.

Seal An object carved with a special design, used to stamp official documents to prove that they have been issued by the owner of the seal.

Taster An official whose job is to taste every dish before it is offered to a ruler, in case someone has poisoned it.

Index